LIES

My Teacher Told Me

The True History of the War for

SOUTHERN INDEPENDENCE

And Other Essays

Clyde N. Wilson

Produced in the Republic of South Carolina by

SHOTWELL PUBLISHING LLC
Post Office Box 2592
Columbia, So. Carolina 29202

WWW.SHOTWELLPUBLISHING.COM

Cover design by Boo Jackson Designs.

ISBN-13: 978-0692613283

ISBN-10: 0692613285

COMMENTS ON CLYDE WILSON'S WRITINGS:

Clyde Wilson had been ploughing the ground long before many of us came to plant. – Donald Livingston

Clyde Wilson is a national treasure. – Alice Teller

Clyde Wilson shows great ability in the field of intellectual history. – American Historical Review

Clyde Wilson is certainly the biggest intellectual heavyweight with the neo-Confederate scene. – Southern Poverty Law Center

. . . a careful scholar who has thought hard and deep about his beloved South. Wilson is, in short, an exemplary historian who displays formidable talent. – Eugene Genovese

. . . a mind as precise and expansive as an encyclopedia . . . These are the same old preoccupations given new life and meaning by a real mind---as opposed to what passes for minds in the current intellectual establishment. – Thomas H. Landess

. . . Clyde Wilson's essays . . . places him on the same level with all the unreconstructed greats in modern Southern letters: Donald Davidson, Andrew Lytle, Frank L. Owsley, Richard Weaver, and M.E. Bradford. – Joseph Scotchie

Clyde Wilson is an obstreperous soldier in the great Jacobin wars that have plagued the nation. – Robert C. Cheeks

PUBLISHER'S NOTE

IN 2015 THE JIHAD AGAINST everything Southern has been artificially revved up again, with even more malice and less sense than before. For war-weary sons and daughters of Dixie and our friends everywhere we offer this antidote—a sample of lots more unreconstructed fare from SHOTWELL PUBLISHERS.

THE SOUTH IS A GARDEN. It has been worn out by the War, Reconstruction, the Period of Desolation, the Depression and the worst ravages of all — Modernity; yet, a worn-out garden, its contours perceived by keen eyes, the fruitfulness of its past stored in memory, can be over time, a time which will last no longer than those of us who initially set our minds to the task, restored, to once again produce, for the time appointed unto it, the fruits which nurture the human spirit and which foreshadow the Garden of which there will be no end.

— Dr. Robert M. Peters of Louisiana

TABLE OF CONTENTS

I DID NOT BELIEVE more than I ever had, that the nation would unite indefinitely behind any Southerner. One reason the country could not rally behind a Southern president, I was convinced, was that the metropolitan press of the Eastern Seaboard would never permit it. My experience in office had confirmed this reaction. I was not thinking just of the derisive articles about my style, my clothes, my manner, my accent, and my family — although I admit I received enough of that kind of treatment in my first few months as President to last a lifetime. I was also thinking of a more deep-seated and far-reaching attitude — a disdain for the South that seems to be woven into the fabric of Northern experience. This is a subject that deserves a more profound explanation than I can give it here — a subject that has never been sufficiently examined.

— President Lyndon B. Johnson

LIES MY TEACHER TOLD ME: THE TRUE HISTORY OF THE WAR FOR SOUTHERN INDEPENDENCE

IN THIS AGE OF POLITICAL CORRECTNESS there has never been a greater need and greater opportunity to refresh our understanding of what happened in America in the years 1861–1865 and start defending our Southern forebears as strongly as they ought to be defended. There is plenty of true history available to us. It is our job to make it known.

All the institutions of American society, including nearly all Southern institutions and leaders, are now doing their best to separate the Confederacy off from the rest of American history and push it into one dark little corner labelled "Slavery and Treason." Being taught at every level of the educational system is the official party line that everything good that we or anyone believe about our Confederate ancestors is a myth, and by myth they mean a pack of lies that Southerners thought up to excuse their evil deeds and defeat.

It was not always so. Franklin D. Roosevelt, Harry Truman, and Jimmy Carter were not ashamed to be photographed with a Confederate flag. Dwight Eisenhower wrote a letter rebuking and correcting someone who had called R.E. Lee a traitor. In the newsreels of World War II and Korea our flag can be seen painted on fighter planes and flying over Marine tents. In the first half of the 20th century every single big Hollywood star played an admirable Confederate character in the movies at least once.

Those days are gone forever as you well know, although I doubt if you know how really bad it is. When we had the controversy over the flag in South Carolina in 2000, some 90 or more historians issued a statement declaring that the war was about slavery and nothing but slavery and that all contrary ideas are invalid. They claimed that this was not simply their opinion, it was irrefutable fact established by them as experts in history. They did not put it exactly this way, but they were saying that our ancestors were despicable and that you and I are stupid and deluded in thinking well of them.

There are a hundred different things wrong with this statement. These historians are not speaking from knowledge or evidence; they are merely expressing the current fashion in historical interpretation. It is a misuse of history, indeed an absurdity, to reduce such a large and complex event as the War for Southern Independence to such simplistic and self-righteous terms. Historical interpretations change over time. Fifty years ago the foremost American historians believed that the war was primarily about economic interests and that slavery was a lesser issue. Fifty years from now, if people are still permitted to voice ideas that differ from the official government party line, historians will be saying something else.

Remember this. History is human experience and you do not have to be an "expert" to have an opinion about human experience. Furthermore, the kindergarten lesson of history is that human experience can be seen from more than one perspective. Never let yourself be put down by a so-called expert who claims to know more about your ancestors than you do. The qualities needed for understanding history are not some special expertise, but are the same qualities you look for in a good juror — the ability to examine all the evidence and weigh it fairly.

And history is not some disembodied truth. All history is the story of somebody's experience. It is somebody's history. When we talk about the War it is our history we are talking about, it is a part of our identity. To tell libellous lies about our ancestors is a direct attack on who we are.

It is right and natural for all people to honour their forefathers. We have every right to honour our Confederate forebears because they are ours, but there is more to it than that. We Southerners are especially fortunate in our forefathers. They not only won a place in the hearts of us, their descendants. They also won the lasting admiration of everyone in the civilized world who values an indomitable spirit in defence of freedom. That is why our battle-flag, which is being suppressed in this country, appeared spontaneously at the fall of the Berlin Wall and among peoples celebrating their liberation from communism.

Our Confederates are admired by the world to a degree seldom granted to lost causes. I find that thoughtful Europeans speak respectfully of the Confederacy, as did Winston Churchill. Foreigners have a great advantage in judging the right and wrong of the War Between the States. They do not automatically assume that everything Yankees do and say is righteous, true, and unselfish. They view Yankees without the rose-coloured glasses with which Yankees view themselves.

The most basic simple fact about the War is that it was a war of invasion and conquest. Once you get clear on this basic fact, everything else falls into place. This is no secret. It is plain in the record. The rulers of the North openly declared that it was a war of conquest, to crush and punish disobedience to government, to create a powerful centralised state, and to keep the South as a captive source of wealth for Northern business and politicians. Lincoln's pretty words about saving government of, by, and for the people are window dressing and the exact opposite of the truth. This is not preserving the Union. It is using war to turn the Union into something else that it was not meant to be.

The U.S. government, under the control of a minority party, launched a massive invasion of the South. They destroyed the democratic, legitimate, elected governments of fourteen States, killed as many of our forefathers as they could, deprived them of their citizenship, subjected them to military occupation, and did many other things that no American, North or South, could previously have imagined were possible.

Though they had four times our resources, they were not able to defeat our men, so the U.S. government launched an unprecedentedly brutal war of terrorism again Southern women and children, white and black. The war was so unpopular in the North that thousands of people were imprisoned by the army without due process, elections were conducted at bayonet point, and they had to import 300,000 foreigners to fill up the army.

This was the war—a brutal war of conquest and occupation against the will of millions of Americans. Was the reason for this the righteous desire to free the slaves?

Not hardly.

I want to talk about the Constitution and the rights of the States as our forefathers understood them. No subject in American history has been more neglected or dealt with more trivially and dishonestly, and yet there are not many subjects in American history that are more important. The more one studies it, the clearer it becomes that our forefathers were right. The Southern understanding of the Constitution has never been refuted. It can't be. It was simply crushed.

According to the Declaration of Independence, governments rest on the consent of the people, who may alter or abolish them when they no longer serve their rightful ends. This is the bedrock American principle.

In every system there must be, at least in theory, a sovereign—a final authority for the settlement of all questions. All Americans are agreed that the people are sovereign. (Actually the people are not sovereign any more, which is part of the tragedy of our lost cause. Sovereignty is now exercised by the President and the Supreme Court.)

But if we say, as earlier Americans did, that the people are sovereign, what do we mean by the people? Our forefathers had a very clear answer to this. State rights was not, despite what they will tell you, something that was made up to defend slavery. It was the most honoured American tradition, implicit in the way the United States Constitution was set up and made valid. The right of the people of a State to exercise their sovereign will and secede from the Union was taken for granted at the Founding of the United States.

James Madison, called the Father of the Constitution, said that the Constitution should be interpreted according to the opinion of the people of the states when they ratified it, and that the Tenth Amendment, which limited the government to specific powers and left all others to the states and the people, was the cornerstone of the Constitution. Just before his election as President Thomas Jefferson drafted the Kentucky Resolutions which stated in absolutely clear language that sovereignty rested in the people of each state. He maintained this before, during, and after he was President. (I know of a case where a graduate student wrote about Jefferson's and Madison's position on State rights. A tenured professor of American history at a large state university told the student that he had made it up because it couldn't be true. Remember this when you hear "expert" professors laying down the law about history.)

Even Alexander Hamilton, the greatest advocate of a strong central government, stated that the government would never have any right to coerce a State. Jefferson in his later years took it for granted that the Union would break up — probably into eastern and western confederacies. There was nothing wrong with that. The sacred thing was not the Union but the consent of the people, which might be better represented in two or three confederacies rather than one. What, after all, is wrong with Americans creating other Unions if that is what the people want?

If time allowed I could give you quotations from now until Christmas proving that the right of secession was clearly understood at the establishment of the Constitution and for long after. But let me try to illustrate my point.

In 1720 the people of South Carolina, acting through their own legislature and militia, exercised their sovereign will by declaring themselves independent of the Lords Proprietors who claimed to own their territory. In 1775, acting in the same exercise of their sovereign will, they threw out the King's government and became an independent nation. And they made this good well before the joint

Declaration of Independence by defeating a British attack on Charleston. In 1787 the people through a convention specially elected to express their sovereign will considered whether or not to ratify the United States Constitution. If you believe that government rests on the consent of the people, then this is the only place the consent could be given. And it was an entirely free act of a sovereign who could say yea or nay without responsibility to any other authority. They ratified the Constitution under the understanding that they were joining in a Union that would be of mutual benefit to all the partners. This was the will of the only sovereign, the people of each State.

In 1860, the people of South Carolina assembled once more in a convention and repealed their previous ratification of the Constitution, which as a sovereign people they were entitled to do. They were now once more an independent nation as they had been before they had given their consent to the Union. They did this because the Union was no longer to their benefit but had become a burden and a danger. They said: We have acted in good faith and been very patient. But obviously you people in control of the federal government intend permanently to exploit our wealth and interfere in our affairs. Our contract with you no longer serves it purpose of mutual benefit and is hereby dissolved.

As you know, our North Carolina people did not want to bring on a crisis. They did not rush into secession, though they were never in doubt about their right. Then Lincoln announced that the legitimate governments of the seven seceded States were not States at all but are merely what he called "combinations of lawbreakers." According to him, the act of the people was merely a crime problem. Once you had accepted the federal government the consent of the people could never be exercised again. He ordered the States to disperse within 30 days and obey his authority, or else. The issue was now clear for our State and the sovereign people of North Carolina elected a convention that unanimously seceded from affiliation with the United States.

Our forefathers were right, and they knew they were right. Their Lost Cause was a loss for all Americans and for the principle that governments must rest on the consent of the people. Imagine for a moment how different our situation would be today if we were able to get together and disobey the federal government which has usurped our right to consent to our rulers.

But I am of good cheer. One of the bad South-hating historians recently whined in print that even though he and other brilliant experts have declared the truth over and over, people still continue to admire the Confederacy and honour that mythical Lost Cause. Why, people still write novels and songs about Lee and even about his horse! Why doesn't anyone write about Grant and his men like that? That they can't understand this tells you what kind of people they are.

Here is our great advantage. Our Confederate ancestors are truly admirable, and decent people all over the world know it. Let's always remember that.

(Speech to the North Carolina Sons of Confederate Veterans)

AMERICA'S RED-HEADED STEPCHILD

ARE YOU PUZZLED AND IRRITATED by the viciousness and falsity of most of what is being published these days about the South and Southern history? The beginning of all wisdom on this subject is to know that in American public speech and so-called scholarship there is usually no effort to understand the South, like any other human phenomenon, as it is. Rather the South is raw material in a morality play about American, that is, about Northern righteousness.

The South is the red-headed stepchild in the American story. Or as Thomas Landess has put it, the South is a swarthy villain who threatens to carry off the fair maiden America unless she is suppressed by the blond hero of the North.

My favourite example of this was a statement a few years ago by an Ivy League intellectual. America, he said, is threatened by increasing violence because of the spread of the "Southern gun culture." This was written at the time of Timothy McVeigh from New York and the U.S. Army, the Unabomber from Harvard and Berkeley, and the Columbine shooters—none of whom were Southern or, except for the latter, used guns.

You see the assumption guiding this great thinker. If there is evil in America it must be because it is oozing out from Dixie, known to good people as the source of all evil in an otherwise pure and righteous country. The distorted thinking, the hatred, and the projection of evil onto others are evident. Unfortunately, much of the history of the South is being written today by people who accept without question the unexamined and self-flattering assumptions of this person.

Another story to get at my point. In 2000, when the controversy of the Confederate flag on the South Carolina capitol was raging, I read that the students at the University of Washington State, out on the Pacific, were rioting over the flag. I daresay that a Southerner can go for months without even thinking about Washington State (though I did enjoy the trip with my children to see the whales in Puget Sound). A Southerner would never be so presumptuous and unneighbourly as to attempt to dictate to the people of Washington State, but they feel it is their right to discern our faults and correct them. We are talking about two different national characters here.

The young son of a family I know, museum-quality specimens of Midwestern liberals, recently wrote to the President about the oil situation. Mr. President, he said, you should do away with cars and make everyone ride horses. However much a Southerner might prefer horses to gas-guzzlers, it would never occur to one of us that the first thing to do was to demand that the government undertake universal enforcement of our preference. This is normal behaviour for a Yankee and is even considered a mark of superior virtue and intelligence.

I could cite a thousand examples of how all this strange mentality vents itself among historians who at the present time have distorted not only Southern, but American and African-American history to the point of pervasive falsification.

In the 1830s a publisher called Jonathan Elliot collected and brought out a work called *Debates in the Ratification Conventions of the Several States on the U.S. Constitution.* At that time very little documentation about the formation of the Constitution was available. A well-known American historian once told me that the publication of "Elliot's Debates" was part of a States' Rights conspiracy by John C. Calhoun. Elliott was not a Southerner and his work was good scholarship that made available some authentic documents about vital matters that ought to have been welcomed by anyone. But since the thrust of the documents supported the Southern view of the Constitution, their publication was obviously evilly motivated. This is the explanation that fit his unconscious Bad-South scenario of American history.

Another example: Historians have been at great pains to explain why South Carolina was so exercised about the tariff that it defied the federal government by Nullification. Why were they so hot and bothered about this unimportant matter? They must have really been crazed with fear of their slaves, or they were lashing out because of their anxiety over soil exhaustion and population loss. Historians can't accept what they plainly said: that they were tired of being ripped off by federal legislation that picked their pockets to benefit some rich people at the North, that they could prove that this was the real economic effect of the tariff, and that they thought the Union should be of mutual benefit to all rather than a burden to some and benefit to others. But since we know that Southerners, unlike Northerners, are always up to no good and we can't believe anything they say, we have to find the hidden cause.

A common trick of the falsifiers is to neglect to ask the question—compared to what? For instance, it is commonplace to assert, without any real evidence, that the antebellum South was dominated by a few of the wealthiest slaveholders who lorded it over the rest of the population. Granted that rich people have more say so in any society than poor people, we ought to ask the question: did the wealthy in the Old South have more power than the wealthy in the North or Europe? Or less power? Or the same amount? It is never even felt necessary to ask the question. We announce that we have found something in the South that we don't like; ergo, we are free to assert that this bad thing particularly characterizes the South.

The current fad is to treat everything good that Southerners say about the Confederacy as part of a "Lost Cause Myth" that Southerners made up after the fact to rationalize their failure and their evilly motivated attempt to destroy the greatest government on earth. Robert E. Lee was not really a great general, Confederate soldiers were not really brave and out-numbered, the people really did not support the Confederacy, a distinct Southern culture was merely a pretence to defend slavery, etc., etc., etc. In the face of vast contradictory evidence, it is simply declared that everything positive Southerners said about themselves was a lie they made up and told after the fact. A catalogue I picked up just a few days ago reported new books: "The Myth of Jefferson Davis" and "The Myth of Bedford Forrest." You see, Southerners always make up flattering stories about themselves while Northerners just tell the true facts.

Southerners are intrinsically evil and Northerners intrinsically good. The South is not to be understood for itself, as it is and was, as something with its own life and identity. It exists only as the bad side of America.

THE TREASURY OF COUNTERFEIT VIRTUE

"O wad some Pow'r the giftie gie us
To see oursels as others see us!"

—Robert Burns

NOT LONG AGO, a well-known conservative historian lamented that the American public had not been morally engaged to undergo sacrifice after the 9/11 attacks, unlike their heroic predecessors after Fort Sumter and Pearl Harbor.

Wait a minute. Pearl Harbor and 9/11 were massive sneak attacks by foreign enemies. The reduction of Fort Sumter was preceded by a gentlemanly warning, was bloodless, and the garrison was allowed to depart with honour. It would not have happened at all if Lincoln had not dissimulated about re-enforcements. Think about this. Why should Southerners (free Americans) permit a fort that had been built with their tax money for their protection to be used as a base to conquer and extort taxes from them? When every other federal post in the South had already been peacefully surrendered pending a *political* settlement. One can become outraged at Fort Sumter only by placing a higher value on the will of the political party controlling the machinery of government than on the core purpose of a free regime to protect the people.

Nor did Lincoln's call after Fort Sumter for 75,000 troops to suppress "the rebellion" at all evoke American unity and determination like that after Pearl Harbor. The call for troops was illegal and the 75,000 was either a deliberate deception or the most terrible mistake in American history, since over a million men were eventually required to complete the conquest of the Southern people and the destruction of their self-government. The immediate effect of Lincoln's mobilization was to drive four more states out of the Union, put the Border States into bloody play, and require military rule in much of the North such as was unprecedented in American experience. And ultimately to require systematic terrorism against non-combatants that is still a source of shame for all decent Americans. It is true Lincoln got a temporary boost of morale from having forced the Confederacy to "fire on the flag," but that did not last. The number of Northern men who evaded service in Mr. Lincoln's war in one way or another was in the hundreds of thousands, and more Northerners voted against him in 1864 than had in 1860, even though the army was used to control the polls.

One wonders that the historian mentioned would even allow Southerners to fight beside real Americans in later wars since he equates Lee and Jackson with Tojo and Bin Laden. Perhaps it has always been this way in Boston, which happens to be the location of the scholar referred to. But in general it has not always been so. Franklin Roosevelt had no objection to being photographed with Confederate flags. Harry Truman chose a romantic equestrian portrait of Lee and Jackson for the lobby of his Presidential Library. Dwight Eisenhower went out of his way to correct someone who called Lee a "traitor," and John Kennedy chose Calhoun as one of the five greatest Senators.

For a long time, Americans North and South observed a Truce. It was agreed that The War was a great tragedy with good and bad on both sides, from which a stronger and better country had emerged. In this scenario, Lincoln is the great martyred Peacemaker who would have "bound up the nation's wounds" and avoided the evils that followed armed conflict. This is a dubious proposition, but one in which it was useful for all parties to believe.

As Southerners well know, things have changed in the last few years. There is a concerted effort to banish the South into one dark little corner of American history labelled "slavery" and "treason." For our purposes here in the Lincoln bicentennial, we can note that there has been an accompanying literature that celebrates Lincoln not as the Peacemaker but as the great Conquering Revolutionary who used any means to eliminate evil and promote change. Which accompanies and justifies America's turn toward a mission to impose "global democracy" by unlimited force and pre-emptive war. Even General Sherman is once more being celebrated as a great military hero for his ruthless campaigns against civilians. (There has been a counter-trend, exemplified not only by Thomas DiLorenzo's and Ronald and Donald Kennedy's best-selling books but by a number of solid monographs exploring the uglier aspects of Northern motives and actions in The War. If my email correspondence from above the Potomac and Ohio is any measure, a great many non-Southern Americans now regard Lincoln as the fount of the excessive centralisation and the aggressive war that they deplore.)

In 1961, during the Civil War centennial, Robert Penn Warren published a little book called *The Legacy of the Civil War*. He had some critical things to say about the tendency of his fellow Southerners to use The War as an excuse to avoid remedying their shortcomings. But for our purposes, what he had to say about the American majority is more pertinent. The éclat of having "saved the Union" and freed the slaves had left Northerners with "a Treasury of Virtue." This is a kind of plenary indulgence that automatically pre-justifies the motives of American violence and the goodness inherent in America's acts to force the world into conformity with its ideal version of itself. Decide for yourself the degree of truth in Warren's observation as it applies to the current American posture in the world.

The Treasury of Virtue renders Americans immune to a simple truth. The War was a war of conquest. It was not a righteous crusade or a family spat. Government of the people would not have suffered if a war of coercion had not been launched against the Southern people. The opposite is true. The purpose of the war was fundamentally to protect the prosperity of the ruling elements of the Northern states by keeping the South captive as a market and a source of raw materials and exports. The primary result of the Republican Party victory was permanent instalment of Hamilton's blessings — a national debt, a protected market for industrialists, and a collusion between bankers and politicians.

Orestres Brownson, a strong supporter of the Union, lamented afterwards that the war had not been sustained by patriotism — but by patronage, profit, and a trumped up hatred of Southerners. Northern support for Lincoln was not nearly as widespread and fervent as our Boston historian would have it. Recent study has raised doubt as to whether Lincoln could have maintained his armies if there had not been widespread industrial unemployment at the beginning of the war, an immense expenditure on enlistment bounties, and unlimited access to foreign recruits.

Since the mid-20th century Americans have been obsessed with race and it has become *de rigueur* to declare that The War was about slavery and nothing but slavery. Earlier generations knew better. Emancipation of the slaves was not a purpose but a by-product of the conquest of the South. The mass of the Northern public and army was far more anti-black than it was anti-slavery, and the destruction of the South was as hard or harder on the black population than on the white. The notion that soldiers in blue and emancipated slaves rushed into each other's arms with shouts of Hallelujah is pure fantasy. Nor was slavery (domestic servitude) in 1860 at all the horror that it is now imagined to be. In 1860 in New York City there were women and children working 16 hour days for starvation wages, 150,000 unemployed, 40,000 homeless, 600 brothels (some with girls as young as 10), and 9,000 grog shops where the poor could temporarily drown their sorrows. A Southern planter who reflected on the circumstances in which he had been born, observed the everyday life around him, and examined his Christian conscience, saw no reason to forever meekly accept the hatred and abuse of strangers who claimed moral authority over him.

In American tradition and understanding, secession should have been an occasion for Constitutional negotiations such as the Confederate government sought, especially by a President whose position, ambiguous and two-faced as it was, had the support of less than 40 per cent of the people. Instead, Lincoln declared that the solemn, constitutional, democratic acts of the people of eleven States were merely combinations of criminals too numerous to be put down by the marshals. He supported his position by a false American history and the transparent lie that the "people" did not really support their States. That day the Constitution died as a governing document for the people and their statesman. It became a mere rule of thumb for politicians and lawyers, who continue Lincoln's heritage of twisting it to suit their ends. After all, the Constitution defines rebellion against the United States as waging war against "them," not as resisting the government. It was Lincoln who was engaged in a rebellion to overthrow the Union. He had to dispense with the real Constitution because it not only disallowed a war of coercion against Americans but also most of the acts of central power in favour of private profit that his party was determined to make permanent.

In fact, Lincoln's campaign to "retake the seditious states" could only rest on the tacit assumption that the Southern states, their land, resources, and people, were and always had been the property of the federal government; or more properly, of the politicians who had got control of the federal machine. And that the South existed not for itself as a self-governing part of America but for the benefit and disposition of the North. The consent of the people could only be given one time and ever after they were bound to obey to the federal machine. Thus the primary principle of the Declaration, that governments rest on the consent of the governed, was abolished. The Union was not preserved and it could not have been under such assumptions, any more than a marriage can be properly preserved by battery. It was changed into something else.

Lincoln's pretty words in the Gettysburg Address managed to have it both ways—he was, he claimed, preserving the sacred old Union and at the same time promulgating a new birth of freedom that was somehow necessary to save government of the people. But these were not the arguments normally used by the spokesmen of his party to justify their war. They spoke instead of conquest and authority and punishment of disobedience to their designs. This is not a Southern accusation, it is the overwhelming evidence of their own words, both public and private. Karl Marx agreed enthusiastically with Lincoln's interpretation of the Declaration of Independence, proclaiming the war to be a rebellion of "slave drivers" against the "one great democratic republic whence the first Declaration of the Rights of Man was issued." Karl Marx also regarded it as a rebellion against progressive German immigrants who somehow were better Americans than the Southern sons of patriots and founders.

It is unlikely, but if Americans could ever come to recognise and admit how much counterfeit is contained in their Treasury of Virtue, then they could have a more realistic view of themselves and play a more humble and responsible role in the world.

(From Chronicles Magazine)

WHAT TO SAY ABOUT DIXIE?

WHAT TO SAY IN BRIEF COMPASS ABOUT THE SOUTH? —a subject that is worthy of the complete works of a Homer, a Shakespeare, or a Faulkner. The South is a geographical, historical, and cultural reality that has provided a crucial source of identity for millions of people for three centuries. Long before there was an entity known as "the United States of America." there was the South. Possibly, there will still be a Southern people long after the American Empire has collapsed upon its hollow shell.

One fine historian defined the South as "not quite a nation within the nation, but the next thing to it." The late M.E. Bradford, whose genial spirit watches over us even now, defined the South as "a vital and long-lasting bond, a corporate identity assumed by those who have contributed to it." This is, characteristically, a broad and generous definition. He proceeded to illustrate that when visualizing the South, he always thought "of Lee in the Wilderness that day when his men refused to let him assume a position in the line of fire and tugged at the bridle of Traveler until they had turned him aside." This was clearly a society at war, not a government military machine.

The South is larger and more salient in population, territory, historical import, distinctive folkways, music, and literature than many of the separate nations of the earth. Were the South independent today, it would be the fourth or fifth largest economy in the world. Citizens of Minneapolis consider themselves cultured because of their Japanese-conducted symphony that plays European music, and assume that the Nashville geniuses who create music all the world loves are rubes and hayseeds. New Yorkers pride themselves on their literary culture. Yet in the second half of the 20th century, if you subtract Southern writers, American literature would be on par with Denmark or Bulgaria and somewhere below Norway and Rumania.

Southerners are the most regionally loyal citizens of the United States. But paradoxically—or perhaps not—they have traditionally been the most loyal to the country at large, ready to repel insult or injury without the need to be dragooned by any ridiculous folderol about saving Haiti or Somalia for democracy. Southerners have given freely to the Union and generally avoided the demands for entitlements that now characterize American life. But their loyalty has been severely tested, especially considering all they have ever asked in return is to be left alone.

Southerners have less reason to be loyal to the collective enterprise of the United States than does any group of citizens. The South was invaded, laid waste, and conquered when it tried to uphold the original and correct understanding of the Declaration of Independence and the Constitution. It took 22 million Northerners, aided by the entire plutocracy and proletariat of the world, four years of the bloodiest warfare in American history and the most unparalleled terrorism against civilians, to subdue five million Southerners—all followed by the horror of Reconstruction. During this entire period, "the Northern conservatives" never opposed the

21

smallest obstacle to the devastations of the radicals. In fact, the Northern "conservatives" have never, in the course of American history, conserved anything.

Since the War, the South has been a colonial possession, economically and culturally, to whatever sleazy elements have been able to exercise national power. A major theme of the American media and popular culture is ridicule and contempt for everything Southern. A major theme of American historical writing is the portrayal of the South as the unique repository of evil in a society that is otherwise shining and pure.

A severely condensed but essentially accurate interpretation of American history could be stated thusly. There are two kinds of Americans. There are those who want to be left alone to pursue their destiny, restrained only by tradition and religion: and those whose identity revolves around compelling others to submit to their own manufactured vision of the good society.

These two aspects of American culture were formed in the 17th century, by the Virginians and Yankees, respectively. The Virginians moved into the interior of America and carved their farms and plantations out of the wilderness. Their goal was to re-create the best of English rural society. They merged with even more vigorous and independent people, the Scots-Irish, to form what is still the better side of the American character.

The Yankees of Massachusetts lived in villages with preacher and teacher. They viewed themselves as a superior, chosen people, a City upon a Hill. As far as they were concerned, they were the true Americans and the only Americans that counted, ignoring or slandering other Americans relentlessly—a sentiment persisting to this day.

The days of Jefferson and Jackson illustrate the freedom and honour underlying America when ruled by the South. During their eras, Virginians gave away their vast Western empire for the joint enjoyment of all Americans, (thus making possible the Midwest and West) and laboured to erect a limited, responsible government. The New Englanders, during the same periods, demanded a reserve of lands for themselves in Ohio; instituted a national bank and funding system by which their money-men profited off the blood of the Revolution; passed the Alien and Sedition laws to essentially enforce their own narrow ideological code on others; opposed the Louisiana Purchase; and demanded tariffs to protect their industries at others' expense. All of which was done in the name of "Americanism."

This profiteering through government, which John Taylor of Caroline called the "paper aristocracy," has always been accompanied by moral imperialism and assumptions of superiority that are even more offensive than the looting. It is from this that the South seceded. It is this combination of greed and moralism which constitutes the Yankee legacy, gives the American empire whatever legitimacy it can claim, and fuels the never-ending reconstruction of society. That is why we use Marines for social work, so that our leaders can congratulate themselves on their moral posture. That is why every town in the land is burdened with empty parking spaces bearing the symbol of the empire, so that the Connecticut Yankee George Bush can posture over his charity to the disabled. That is why, right now, wealthy Harvard University receives from the treasury a 200 percent overhead bonus on its immense federal grants, while the impoverished University of South Carolina receives only 50 percent of its much smaller bounty.

The term American is an abstraction without human content — it refers, at best, to a government, territory, standard of living, and a set of dubious and dubiously observed propositions. It refers to nothing akin to values or culture, nothing that represents the humanness of human beings. It could be reasonably argued that there is no such thing as an American people, although we have persuaded ourselves there was when shouldering the burdens of several wars. There was perhaps a time in the mid-twentieth century when an American nationality might have emerged naturally. But that time has passed with the onslaught of new immigrants.

Unlike the term American, when we say Southern, we know we imply a certain history, literature, music, and speech; particular folkways, attitudes and manners; a certain set of political responses and pieties; and a traditional view of the proper dividing line between the private and the public. Things which are unique, easily observable, and have continued over many generations.

The bloody St. Andrews cross of the Confederacy is a symbol throughout the world of heroic resistance to oppression — except in the U.S., where it is in the process of suppression. Southerners are democratic in spirit, but they have never made a fetish of democracy and certainly not of what Mel Bradford called "Equality." With T.S. Eliot, Southerners intuitively recognize that democracy is a procedure and not a substitute for an authentic social fabric. However free and equal we may be, we are nothing without a culture, and there is no culture without religion.

The South, many believe, still has a substantial authentic culture, both high and folk, and it still has a purchase on Christianity. That is, the South is a civilizational reality in a sense which the United States is not, and it will last longer than the American Empire.

For a long time, we have been asking what the South can do for the United States. A proper question to now ask is what can the United States do for the South? The Union is nothing except for its constituent parts. The Union is good and just to the degree that it fosters its authentic parts. That is precisely why our forefathers made the Constitution and the Union and gave consent, voluntarily, to them — to enhance themselves, not the government.

As the Southern poet Allen Tate pointed out, the wrong turn was taken in the War Between the States when the United States ceased living by the Southern conception of a limited partnership and became instead a collection of buildings in Washington from which orders of self-justifying authority were issued. The great classical scholar and Confederate Soldier Basil Gildersleeve remarked that the War was a conflict over grammar — whether the proper grammar was "the United States are" or "the United States is." We have been using the wrong grammar.

The South's lost political legacy was laid out by Rev. Robert Lewis Dabney, Presbyterian theologian and Stonewall Jackson's chief of staff, several years following the War. Echoing Calhoun, he said:

> Government is not the creator but the creature of human society. The Government has no mission from God to make the community, on the contrary the community is determined by Providence, where it is happily determined for us by far other causes than the meddling of governments — by historical causes in the distant past, by vital ideas, propagated by great individual minds — especially by the church and its doctrines. The only communities which have had

their characters manufactured for them by governments have had a villainously bad character. Noble races make their governments. Ignoble ones are made by them.

The United States was created to serve the communities which make it up, not for the communities to serve the government. That is what the South and all authentic American communities need to recapture from a ruling class bent upon constantly remaking us. If we recapture that, we will again be citizens giving our consent to the necessary evil of a limited government, and not the serfs and cannon fodder of the American Empire.

ABOUT THE AUTHOR

DR CLYDE WILSON is Distinguished Professor Emeritus of History of the University of South Carolina, where he served from 1971 to 2006. He holds a Ph.D. from the University of North Carolina at Chapel Hill. He recently completed editing of a 28-volume edition of *The Papers of John C. Calhoun* which has received high praise for quality. He is author or editor of a more than a dozen other books and over 600 articles, essays, and reviews in a variety of books and journals, and has lectured all over the U.S and in Europe, many of his lectures having been recorded online and on CDs and DVDs. Dr Wilson directed 17 doctoral dissertations, a number of which have been published. Books written or edited include *Why the South Will Survive, Carolina Cavalier: The Life and Mind of James Johnston Pettigrew, The Essential Calhoun*, three volumes of *The Dictionary of Literary Biography* on American historians, *From Union to Empire: Essays in the Jeffersonian Tradition, Defending Dixie: Essays in Southern History and Culture*, and *Chronicles of the South*.

Dr Wilson is founding director of the Society of Independent Southern Historians; former president of the St. George Tucker Society for Southern Studies; recipient of the Bostick Prize for Contributions to South Carolina Letters, the first annual John Randolph Society Lifetime Achievement Award, and the Robert E.

Lee Medal of the Sons of Confederate Veterans. He is   M.E. Bradford Distinguished Professor of the Abbeville Institute; Contributing Editor of *Chronicles: A Magazine of American Culture;* founding dean of the Stephen D. Lee Institute, educational arm of the Sons of Confederate Veterans; and co-founder of Shotwell Publishing.

Dr Wilson has two grown daughters, an excellent son-in-law, and two outstanding grandsons. He lives in the Dutch Fork of South Carolina, not far from the Santee Swamp where Francis Marion and his men rested between raids on the first invader.

AVAILABLE FROM SHOTWELL PUBLISHING

IF YOU ENJOYED THIS BOOK, perhaps some of our other titles will pique your interest. The following titles are currently available from Shotwell at Amazon and all major online book retailers.

A Legion of Devils: Sherman in South Carolina by Karen Stokes

Annals of the Stupid Party: Republicans Before Trump by Clyde N. Wilson

Carolina Love Letters by Karen Stokes

Confederaphobia: An American Epidemic by Paul C. Graham

Dismantling the Republic by Jerry C. Brewer

Dixie Rising: Rules for Rebels by James R. Kennedy

Emancipation Hell: The Tragedy Wrought By Lincoln's Emancipation Proclamation by Kirkpatrick Sale

Lies My Teacher Told Me: The True History of the War for Southern Independence by Clyde N. Wilson

Maryland, My Maryland: The Cultural Cleansing of a Small Southern State by Joyce Bennett.

Nullification: Reclaiming Consent of the Governed by Clyde N. Wilson

Punished with Poverty: The Suffering South by James R. & Walter D. Kennedy

Segregation: Federal Policy or Racism? by John Chodes

Southern Independence. Why War?- The War to Prevent Southern Independence by Dr. Charles T. Pace

Southerner, Take Your Stand! by John Vinson

Washington's KKK: The Union League During Southern Reconstruction by John Chodes.

When the Yankees Come: Former South Carolina Slaves Remember Sherman's Invasion. Edited with Introduction by Paul C. Graham

The Yankee Problem: An American Dilemma by Clyde N. Wilson

GREEN ALTAR BOOKS (Literary Imprint)

A New England Romance & Other SOUTHERN Stories by Randall Ivey

Tiller by James Everett Kibler

GOLD-BUG MYSTERIES (Mystery & Suspense Imprint)

To Jekyll and Hide by Martin L. Wilson

ONE LAST THING

IF YOU ENJOYED THIS BOOK or found it useful or informative, we'd be very grateful if you'd post a brief review of it on the vendor's website. To sign-up for new release notification and receive a FREE DOWNLOADABLE EDITION of this book by visiting FreeLiesBook.com or by texting the word "Dixie" to 345345. You can always unsubscribe and keep the book, so you've got nothing to lose!

In the current political and cultural climate, it is important that we get accurate, Southern friendly material into the hands of our friends and neighbours. Your support really can make a difference in helping us unapologetically celebrate and defend our Southern home!

We can be found online at

WWW.SHOTWELLPUBLISHING.COM

THANK YOU FOR YOUR SUPPORT!

Made in the USA
Columbia, SC
22 August 2023

21983627R10024